A LIFEBUILDER

DANIEL

Spiritual Living in a Secular World

12 Studies for individuals or groups

Douglas Connelly

"Reuven, the Master of the Universe blessed me with a brilliant son. . . . Ah, what it is to have a brilliant son! Not a smart son, Reuven, but a brilliant son, a Daniel, a boy with a mind like a jewel."
Chaim Potok, The Chosen

With Notes for Leaders

SCRIPTURE UNION
130 City Road, London ECIV 2NJ

First published in the United States by InterVarsity Press
First published in Great Britain by Scripture Union, 1988
Reprinted 1990 (twice)

ISBN 0 86201 529 4

Cover photograph: Peter French

Printed in England by Ebenezer Baylis & Son Limited, The Trinity Press, Worcester and London

Contents

Getting the Most from LifeBuilder Bible Studies

Many of us long to fill our minds and our lives with Scripture. We desire to be transformed by its message. LifeBuilder Bible Studies are designed to be an exciting, thought-provoking and challenging way to do just that. Their ultimate goal is to help us build our lives on God's Word.

How They Work

LifeBuilder Bible Studies have a number of distinctive features. Perhaps the most important is that they are *inductive* rather than *deductive.* In other words, they lead us to *discover* what the Bible says rather than simply *telling* us what it says.

They are also thought provoking. They help us to think about the meaning of the passage so that we can truly understand what the author is saying. The questions require more than one-word answers.

The studies are personal. Questions expose us to the promises, assurances, exhortations and challenges of God's Word. They are designed to allow the Scriptures to renew our minds so that we can be transformed by the Spirit of God. This is the ultimate goal of all Bible study.

The studies are versatile. They are designed for student, neighborhood and church groups. They are also effective for individual study.

How They're Put Together

LifeBuilder Bible Studies also have a distinctive format. Each study need take no more than forty-five minutes in a group setting or thirty minutes in personal study—unless you choose to take more time.

The studies can be used within a quarter system in a church and fit well in a semester or trimester system on a college campus. If a guide has more than thirteen studies, it is divided into two or occasionally three parts of approximately twelve studies each.

LifeBuilder Bible Studies use a workbook format. Space is provided for writing answers to each question. This is ideal for personal study and allows group members to prepare in advance for the discussion.

The studies also contain leader's notes. They show how to lead a group discussion, provide additional background information on certain questions, give helpful tips on group dynamics and suggest ways to deal with problems which may arise during the discussion. With such helps, someone with little or no experience can lead an effective study.

Suggestions for Individual Study

1. As you begin each study, pray that God will help you to understand and apply the passage to your life.
2. Read and reread the assigned Bible passage to familiarize yourself with what the author is saying. In the case of book studies, you may want to read through the entire book prior to the first study. This will give you a helpful overview of its contents.
3. A good modern translation of the Bible, rather than the King James Version or a paraphrase, will give you the most help. The New International Version, the New American Standard Bible and the Revised Standard Version are all recommended. However, the questions in this guide are based on the New International Version.
4. Write your answers in the space provided in the study guide. This will help you to express your understanding of the passage clearly.
5. It might be good to have a Bible dictionary handy. Use it to look up any unfamiliar words, names or places.

Suggestions for Group Study

1. Come to the study prepared. Follow the suggestions for individual study mentioned above. You will find that careful preparation will greatly enrich your time spent in group discussion.

2. Be willing to participate in the discussion. The leader of your group will not be lecturing. Instead, he or she will be encouraging the members of the group to discuss what they have learned from the passage. The leader will be asking the questions that are found in this guide. Plan to share what God has taught you in your individual study.

3. Stick to the passage being studied. Your answers should be based on the verses which are the focus of the discussion and not on outside authorities such as commentaries or speakers. This guide deliberately avoids jumping from book to book or passage to passage. Each study focuses on only one passage. Book studies are generally designed to lead you through the book in the order in which it was written. This will help you follow the author's argument.

4. Be sensitive to the other members of the group. Listen attentively when they share what they have learned. You may be surprised by their insights! Link what you say to the comments of others so the group stays on the topic. Also, be affirming whenever you can. This will encourage some of the more hesitant members of the group to participate.

5. Be careful not to dominate the discussion. We are sometimes so eager to share what we have learned that we leave too little opportunity for others to respond. By all means participate! But allow others to also.

6. Expect God to teach you through the passage being discussed and through the other members of the group. Pray that you will have an enjoyable and profitable time together.

7. If you are the discussion leader, you will find additional suggestions and helpful ideas for each study in the leader's notes. These are found at the back of the guide.

Introducing Daniel

In the sweep of great world empires, the impact of military conquest on individual people is usually overlooked. For example, the fall of Jerusalem into the hands of Babylon six hundred years before Christ probably did not make much of a stir in the ancient world. It was an event so insignificant to the Babylonians that it wasn't even worth mentioning in their official chronicles.

This was the first of three defeats that those in Judah would suffer from the king of Babylon, Nebuchadnezzar. He simply established Babylonian authority over Judah and left. On the surface not much changed. But behind the scenes some Jewish families and especially some young Jewish men were deeply affected. A number of gifted young men from the families of the Jewish nobility were taken from their homes to a new land. They were thrust into a new lifestyle. Every effort was made to break down their former convictions. They had to make a difficult choice. Would they hold to their faith and to a life of obedience to the Lord God, or would they flow into the new culture? It was a time of crisis for these young men, including the man we will be studying together—Daniel.

It is precisely at this point that we identify with Daniel. Regardless of how sheltered our existence has been as children or how often we were taken to Sunday school, there comes a time when we are thrust into a pagan world. We are confronted in a modern university or on the job or in society with a lifestyle radically different from what is taught in the Bible. At each turn we have to make difficult decisions. Will we obey God regardless of the consequences, or will we become part of the surrounding culture?

Daniel gives us practical and personal help in our struggle. He was a man who rose to a position of great power and prestige in the world system but who never compromised essential biblical principles. He shows us how to live a life of spiritual integrity in the crush of a secular world. Anyone who has been tempted to cave in to such pressures will learn much from him.

The Historical Framework of the Book

Israel's great king Solomon died in 931 B.C. Solomon's son, Rehoboam, foolishly provoked the leaders of the northern part of the nation, and they split off from the south. The northern tribes (ten of them) were called Israel. They existed until 722 B.C. when they were destroyed by the Assyrians. The southern two tribes were called Judah. God spared Judah until 586 B.C. when the Babylonian armies crushed the nation.

Nebuchadnezzar, the Babylonian commander, had come to Judah and Jerusalem twice before to put down Jewish rebellion against the authority of the empire. In 605 B.C. the Jews had been treated fairly well. A few young men (including Daniel) from the leading families had been taken as hostages, but the nation was left relatively undisturbed. In 597 B.C. the treatment was harsher. More people were deported to Babylon, including the king, Jehoiachin, and another prophet, Ezekiel. Finally, in 586 B.C. the Babylonian patience was exhausted. The temple of God was burned, the walls of Jerusalem were broken down, and the people were virtually all killed or deported to Babylon. A summary of these three "conquests" can be found in 2 Kings 24—25 and 2 Chronicles 36.

God judged Judah for seventy years (from 605 B.C. to 536 B.C.)—a period called the Babylonian captivity. In 536 B.C. Babylon was defeated by a new world power, Persia. Cyrus, the Persian ruler, allowed the Jews to return to Judah.

Daniel's ministry in Babylon extended through the entire seventy-year Babylonian captivity and on into the reign of the Persians. Daniel lived well into his eighties or nineties! His primary prophetic focus was on the Gentiles. Even during the period of Judah's humiliation God's voice was heard in the courtroom of the emperor.

The Theological Focus of the Book

If you read the book of Daniel and only see a den of lions and strange visions, you have missed the main character in the book—a sovereign God! Daniel wrote this book not to glorify himself but to exalt the Lord. In every circumstance, in every crisis, Daniel points us to a God who is sovereignly at work in human history.

To say that God is sovereign simply means that nothing happens that is not planned or permitted by God. That is true of kingdoms, and it is true in our lives. Daniel's God is not a weak, frustrated deity who sits in heaven, wringing his hands, hoping everything will turn out right. He is a God who orders all events according to his own will.

The book of Daniel is written in a literary form known as apocalyptic literature. Apocalyptic literature speaks to us in those times when God seems to be absent. The crushed people of Judah in Daniel's day were saying, "Where is God?" Daniel answers their questions by showing them that, even in a national catastrophe, God is working out his purpose and plan.

Daniel is able to resist compromise because of his relationship to a sovereign God. His obedience was simply an expression of God's kingship in his life. Daniel's courage to proclaim God's message came from his allegiance to a sovereign God. He saw the Lord as the one who was King over the earthly kings of Babylon. Be prepared then in this study to see God in a new way! It will be a stretching, convicting, but life-changing adventure.

Daniel and the Future

The second part of the book of Daniel is less well known and markedly more difficult to understand than the first part of the book. But it is no less profitable! In Daniel 1—6 the focus is primarily on the life and character of Daniel as a *man* of God. In Daniel 7—12 the focus is on Daniel as the *messenger* of God. These chapters consist of a series of visions given to Daniel—visions of the future of the gentile nations (chapter 7) and of the nation of Israel (chapters 8—12).

The visions of Daniel are a source of controversy among students of the Bible. The first area of controversy centers around the *integrity* of the visions. Liberal and critical scholars maintain that what is recorded in these chapters is not prophecy at all. Instead the writer wrote after the events (sometime in the second century B.C.) but cast what he wrote in the literary form of predictions given by God to a wise man in Babylon four hundred years earlier. According to this view, these chapters record *history* (a record of events that have already transpired) and not *prophecy* (a prediction of events in the future).

For those who accept the Bible as God's revelation, this controversy is settled by the claims of the book itself and by the defense of those claims mounted by evangelical scholars. We also have Jesus' own confirmation of Daniel. In Matthew 24:15 he referred to Daniel as a real person and called him "the prophet." Jesus quoted from these later chapters of Daniel and took them as authoritative revelation from God (see Mt 24:30; Lk 21:27).

The second area of controversy centers on their *interpretation*. Even those who agree on the historical integrity of Daniel disagree on how these visions should be interpreted. Our objective in this guide is not to defend one particular prophetic system but rather to try to understand what Daniel says. Therefore, while we will refer to other biblical paasages, the emphasis of each study will be on what we can learn from *this* book about God's program for human history. Not all the answers about the future will be found in one part of God's truth. If we understand this part, however, we will have a better understanding of the whole as we attempt to develop a biblical framework for future events. We will gain far more from Daniel if we try to learn what is revealed here rather than seeking to defend a preconceived idea of what we want Daniel to say.

While Daniel 7—12 is not an easy section of Scripture, it is just as much the Word of God as Daniel 1—6 or the Gospel of John or Romans. Therefore, it is profitable to us for instruction and correction. After spending many hours in these chapters, I can tell you that they not only expand our understanding of God's program for the future of the world, they also expand our capacity to trust a sovereign God for *our* future. His cosmic, eternal plan includes us!

1
Have You Got What It Takes?

Daniel 1

How did you feel when you first moved away from home and were launched out on your own? Daniel and his friends were torn from their land and taken to Babylon as young men. They were probably only twelve to fourteen years old. In Babylon they were placed in a three-year training program to prepare them to oversee Jewish affairs in the Babylonian Empire. A crisis of conscience erupted when the first meal was served.

1. Think back to when you first moved away from home. What new adjustments did you have to make?

2. Read Daniel 1. What can you discover from verses 1-2 about the author's perspective on how and why events in our world occur?

3. What specific tactics were used to give these young Jews a new Babylonian orientation (vv. 3-7)?

4. How do these compare with the pressures Christians face in a secular society?

---

5. Why were the food regulations of the Old Testament Law so important to Daniel (vv. 8-10)?

Do you think he was making a big issue out of a minor problem? Explain.

---

6. What criteria can Christians use today to determine which activities we will engage in and which we won't?

---

7. What steps did Daniel take to provide a creative alternative to the king's plan (vv. 11-14)?

---

8. What can we learn from Daniel's attitude and actions when our biblical convictions are challenged?

9. What factors combined to produce the exceptional ability of Daniel and his friends?

---

10. What one aspect of Daniel's character or conduct in this chapter impresses you most?

---

11. How can you follow Daniel's example in your own life?

2
A Disturbing Dream

Daniel 2:1-30

In *The Voyage of the Dawn Treader* C. S. Lewis describes an island where dreams come true. " 'This is the island I've been looking for this long time,' said one of the sailors. . . 'Fools!' said a man from the island, stamping his foot with rage. 'That's the sort of talk that brought me here, and I'd better have been drowned or never born.' " Suddenly every man began rowing as they never had before, "for it had taken everyone just that half-minute to remember certain dreams they had had—dreams that make you afraid to sleep again." In Daniel 2 Nebuchadnezzar had such a dream, a dream that was both troub ling and true.

---

1. Have you ever had a dream that was so real that it almost seemed true? How did you feel when you woke up?

---

2. Read Daniel 2:1-30. Why do you think Nebuchadnezzar demanded to know the content of his dream as well as its interpretation (vv. 1-13)?

3. Imagine that you were in Daniel's situation. How would you and your friends respond if you faced certain death unless you could interpret a dream you knew nothing about?

---

4. What can we learn from Daniel's example about how we should react to a personal crisis (vv. 14-18)?

---

5. What do verses 19-23 tell you about how to respond to answered prayer?

---

6. Verses 20-23 have often been called "Daniel's Psalm." What aspects of God's character are emphasized in these verses?

---

7. How does this knowledge of God's character change your perspective on Daniel's situation in this chapter?

---

8. It is common to feel like we are at the mercy of the people and circumstances around us. How should a knowledge of God's wisdom, sovereignty and power affect our view of the people and circumstances in our lives?

9. How did Daniel's knowledge of God's character reveal itself in his remarks to King Nebuchadnezzar (vv. 27-30)?

---

10. Three aspects of Daniel's spiritual maturity stand out in this chapter: his *wisdom* in response to a crisis, his *prayer* in response to a problem and his *praise* in response to God's work in his life. How can Daniel's example help you grow in one of these areas?

3
The Future from a Divine Perspective

Daniel 2:31-49

Daniel 2 is one of the most amazing prophetic passages in the Bible. It was written in 600 B.C., yet it predicted the future rise and fall of four great world empires! Some of Daniel 2 may seem like so much ancient history to us, but it was *all* future to Daniel. This passage gives us a long look at the sovereign authority of God, who not only has a plan for human history but is also carrying out that plan perfectly.

1. From your study of Daniel so far, summarize the series of events that led up to Daniel's appearance before King Nebuchadnezzar.

2. Read Daniel 2:31-49. As you think about Daniel's description of the dream in verses 31-35 (not the *interpretation* of the dream in later verses), what was it about the dream that may have caused Nebuchadnezzar to be troubled (see v. 1)?

3. The interpretation of the dream begins in verse 36. Why do you think God referred to Nebuchadnezzar as the head of gold (vv. 36-38)?

4. What observations can you make about the relative value and relative strength of the four metals that made up the statue (vv. 31-33)?

5. While Daniel does not say who the future kingdoms are, we can identify them as Medo-Persia (silver), Greece (bronze) and Rome (iron). What does Daniel say about the relative nature and power of these kingdoms (vv. 36-43)?

What is the significance of the mixture of clay (ceramic) with iron (vv. 41-43)?

6. Daniel's predictions were so accurate that some scholars believe the book is not really prophecy but history written after the fact. How would your response to Daniel be different if you believed it was just, as one writer put it, "a pious fraud"?

7. Verse 44 says that "in the time of those kings [the ones represented by the toes?] the God of heaven will set up a kingdom." What characteristics of the kingdom of God are described in verses 44-45?

In your opinion, was this prophecy fulfilled when Christ established the church or is the kingdom still future? Explain.

---

8. What does this chapter teach us about God's activity in the course of human history?

---

9. How can the portrait of God in this chapter encourage us to trust him with our life and circumstances?

---

10. Take time to thank God for his control over the present and the future.

4
Bow or Burn!

Daniel 3

The story of Shadrach, Meshach and Abednego in the fiery furnace ranks with Daniel in the lion's den and David and Goliath as one of the best-known and most exciting Bible stories. One of the problems with a story that's so familiar is that we tend to forget that it really happened. It is not a myth. It is history! It is also a very practical chapter for men and women who are trying to live for God in a secular society. We face the same pressure these three faced—the pressure to compromise what is right before God in order to be accepted by others.

1. In what ways are Christians tempted to compromise in order to be accepted by others?

2. Read Daniel 3. What connection (if any) do you see between this image and Nebuchadnezzar's dream in chapter 2?

What do you think motivated Nebuchadnezzar to build this image of gold (vv. 1-7)?

3. Why do you think the astrologers reported the disobedience of Shadrach, Meshach and Abednego to Nebuchadnezzar (vv. 8-12)?

---

4. What temptations do you think Shadrach, Meshach and Abednego faced when they were brought before the king (vv. 13-15)?

---

5. What impresses you most about their response to these temptations (vv. 16-18)?

---

6. How could you follow their example if you were found to have terminal cancer?

How could their example help if you faced the possibility of losing your job or receiving a poor grade because of your refusal to compromise God's Word?

---

7. Some Christians claim that pain or sickness or trial are always the result of sin or lack of faith. How would you respond to that claim in light of this passage?

8. As you look at Nebuchadnezzar's response (vv. 13-15, 19-23), what evidence do you see that his basic conflict was with God rather than with these three men?

9. What specific actions did God take to bring assurance to the three men and to demonstrate his power to Nebuchadnezzar (vv. 24-30)?

10. As you look back over this chapter, what lessons about the risks and rewards of obedience are most significant to you personally?

11. What commitments can you make to God today that will prepare you to face the pressures of a secular world?

5
The Sovereign God Rules

Daniel 4

We are not accustomed to hearing our national leaders describe their sins in public. That's why Daniel 4 is such an unusual chapter! Nebuchadnezzar, the great, proud, powerful king of Babylon, writes a letter to the world describing in detail how God humiliated him for seven years and then graciously restored him.

1. Think about the proudest person you know. If you were in charge of humbling him or her, how would you go about it?

2. Read Daniel 4. How does Nebuchadnezzar's proclamation in 4:1-3 differ from what he expressed in Daniel 3:28-29?

3. As you read Nebuchadnezzar's description of the dream (vv. 9-18), what aspects of the dream might have caused the king to be "terrified" (v. 5)?

4. Three times in this chapter God's purpose for giving the dream is repeated (vv. 17, 25, 32). Why do you think God was so intent on impressing Nebuchadnezzar with his sovereign authority instead of his grace or his love?

---

5. If we accept verse 17 as applicable today, then must we conclude that Adolf Hitler and Joseph Stalin came to power by God's decree? Explain.

If so, how does that challenge your perception of who God is and how he acts?

---

6. If Nebuchadnezzar had repented of his sins as Daniel advised, do you think God would have withheld his judgment, or was his decision irrevocable at this point (vv. 24-27)? Explain.

---

7. What does the fact that God waited a full year between the announcement of judgment and its actual fulfillment (v. 29) tell us?

---

8. What specific steps did God take to humble Nebuchadnezzar (vv. 31-33)?

9. What does Nebuchadnezzar's experience teach us about the dangers of pride?

---

10. A new Nebuchadnezzar came out on the other end of this experience. Instead of giving himself glory, he gives God glory (vv. 34-37). Do you think he was simply forced into humility by God's iron fist, or was there a genuine change of attitude toward God? Explain.

---

11. Sometimes we gain fresh insight into God's character and ways as we wrestle with a hard aspect of God's truth. What is the hardest thing about this chapter for you to accept?

---

12. What does that hard lesson teach you about how God works in our lives to bring us to Christlikeness?

6
The Handwriting on the Wall

Daniel 5

Never underestimate the influence of one godly life! As chapter 5 opens, Daniel is an old man—more than eighty years old. The successors to Nebuchadnezzar's throne have ignored him. He has been shuffled off into some obscure office in the Babylonian bureaucracy. But when the king finds himself in trouble, he calls for God's man. Daniel shows us how to stand for God over the long haul.

---

1. The Bible is full of good and bad examples. Why is it so important to learn from other people's experiences?

---

2. Read Daniel 5. The chapter begins with a party! As you read verses 1-4, what actions and attitudes on the part of Belshazzar and his guests do you think would have provoked the Lord's anger?

---

3. The events in this chapter take place in 539 B.C., the year (and the very night) of the fall of Babylon to the Medo-Persian army led by Cyrus the Great. The Babylonians considered their city impregnable. They had twenty years of food supplies on hand and the fresh-water Euphrates River flowed through the heart of the city. With that background, what do you think motivated

Belshazzar to have this feast?

4. How would you have reacted if you had been at the banquet and saw a hand appear and write on the wall (v. 5)?

5. Three times Daniel has recorded the failure of the "wise men" of Babylon to interpret the message of God. What point is Daniel trying to make?

6. Why do you think Daniel reminds Belshazzar of how God dealt with Nebuchadnezzar (vv. 18-21)?

7. What insights into the nature of Belshazzar's sins can you find in verses 22-23?

8. In what areas might we be tempted to be proud or arrogant?

9. How can Daniel's words to Belshazzar help us become more humble and thankful to God (vv. 18-24)?

10. Based on what is recorded in verses 29-30, do you think Belshazzar accepted Daniel's interpretation as the authoritative message of the true God? Explain.

---

11. Why do you think Daniel emphasizes that "that very night" the city of Babylon fell and Belshazzar was killed (v. 30)?

---

12. How has this chapter demonstrated that seventy years of life under Babylon's influence had not broken down Daniel's convictions?

---

13. What can we learn from Daniel's example that will help us resist pressures to compromise our convictions?

7
On the Menu at the Lions' Club

Daniel 6

Daniel in the lions' den is a story that we never get tired of hearing. As a child, I was impressed by this story because Daniel was not thrown into the lion's den for being *bad.* He was thrown in for being *godly!* That is an important point to keep in mind as we study. We usually expect that when we do wrong we ought to be punished, and when we do right we ought to be praised. That is certainly the ideal, but it doesn't always work out that way. Sometimes those who do wrong are rewarded, and those who do right are persecuted. This chapter demonstrates that godliness can be costly.

---

1. How would you feel if the people you work with decided to watch everything about your public and private life?

---

2. Read Daniel 6. Why do you think the Persian officials tried to find grounds for charges against Daniel (vv. 1-5)?

3. What do we learn about Daniel's character from the results of the investigation by his enemies?

4. If you were being watched like Daniel was watched, what changes (if any) would you want to make in your present lifestyle?

5. King Darius willingly signed the document prohibiting prayer to anyone but him (vv. 6-9). How does this action resemble the sins of his predecessors?

6. What specific evidences do you find in verse 10 of Daniel's consistent obedience to God?

7. How do verses 14-20 underscore the impact Daniel's life had on the king?

8. In what ways would the miracle Darius witnessed have reinforced Daniel's personal example (vv. 21-24)?

9. How has Daniel encouraged you to be a more Christlike example to those around you?

---

10. What specific aspects of God's character can you discover in Darius's decree praising the Lord "God of Daniel" (vv. 25-27)?

---

11. Think back over the first six chapters. How can the fact that God "holds in his hand your life and all your ways" (5:23) help you to honor and obey him, as Daniel did?

8

A Prophetic Panorama

Daniel 7

Have you ever wondered if there was any order or plan to the course of human history? Nations and empires rise, expand, degenerate and fall. Leaders live, rule and die. But where is everything headed? Some in despair say that human history is going nowhere. Others try to sound optimistic and say that history is going wherever the human race takes it. Christians who know their God and his Word, however, realize that history does have a plan. That's the assurance God gave Daniel in what at first appeared to be a terrifying night vision!

---

1. What are some of the ways that people think the world will come to an end?

---

2. Read Daniel 7. The sea is used in many prophetic passages to represent the nations of the world (see, for example, Is 17:12-13; 57:20 and Lk 21:25). If that is the picture here, how would you explain verses 2-3?

3. Daniel sees four beasts which, according to verse 17, represent four kingdoms. The lionlike appearance of the first beast may represent that kingdom's strength and majesty. What characteristics of the second, third and fourth kingdoms are suggested by verses 5-7?

---

4. What aspects of God's nature and power are suggested by Daniel's description of the Ancient of Days in verses 9-10?

How can this vision of God give us hope and stability when the nations (or our lives) are in turmoil?

---

5. The final figure to appear in Daniel's vision is "one like a son of man" (vv. 13-14)—an apparent description of the Lord Jesus. Why do you think all the kings and kingdoms of the world are pictured as beasts but Christ looks like a son of man?

---

6. After the four kingdom's rise, "the saints of the Most High will receive the kingdom" (vv. 17-18). How is their conquest different from that of the four kingdoms?

7. Describe the political and military power of the "other horn" from the information found in this chapter (vv. 19-26).

8. What is the moral and spiritual character of the "other horn"?

9. Twice the heavenly interpreter emphasizes that the last king will be tried and condemned by God (vv. 22, 26). In your opinion why does God go to the effort of setting up court to judge someone so blatantly sinful?

10. How does reading this passage affect your attitude toward the future?

11. Daniel is told that the saints of the Most High will share in the kingdom with the Son of man. What do you find most appealing about Daniel's description of God's kingdom (vv. 13-14, 27), and why?

9
World Powers in Conflict
Daniel 8

God gave Daniel the unique opportunity of looking at the future. But in chapter 8 that future gets very personal. The first seven chapters stressed the destinies of the gentile world powers. In chapters 8—12, the emphasis is on the destiny of Israel.

1. If God offered to show you glimpses of our nation's future over the next two hundred years, would you want to see them? Explain.

2. Read Daniel 8. Daniel is first given a rather strange vision involving a ram and a goat (vv. 1-14). No interpretation is given until after the scene has passed. Why do you think God chose to communicate future events to Daniel in this way? Why not simply tell him the historical facts?

3. In verse 20 Daniel is told that the ram represents the kings of the Medo-Persian empire. From the events portrayed in verses 3-4, how would you expect this kingdom to come on the world scene?

4. The goat with one large horn is a symbol of the Greek empire and their notable first king, Alexander the Great (v. 21). From the scene in verses 5-8, how would you describe the clash of these two empires?

---

5. From your experience and knowledge gained thus far in the "interpretation of visions" with Daniel as a guide, how would you interpret the symbolism of verses 9-12?

---

6. Compare and contrast the king from Greece (8:9-12, 23-25) with the king from Rome (7:8-12, 24-26).

---

7. The "stern-faced king" (v. 23) whom Gabriel describes is probably Antiochus Epiphanes, who ruled Syria and Palestine from 175 to 164 B.C. He hated the Jews and their God. His most infamous act was desecrating the Temple in Jerusalem in 168 B.C. For just over three years ("2300 evenings and mornings," v. 14), no sacrifices to God were permitted. Finally, the Jews were able to drive Antiochus out of Israel and to reclaim the Temple. If you had been a Jew living under the tyranny of Antiochus, how would it have made you feel to read Daniel's prophetic prediction of the very events you were experiencing?

---

8. Daniel's predictions were fulfilled precisely and literally. Should we expect biblical predictions about our future to be fulfilled in the same way? Explain.

9. Twice (vv. 19, 26) Gabriel makes it clear that this vision concerns (applies to) the "time of the end" or "the distant future." Many Bible scholars believe that Antiochus Epiphanes is a picture of the final evil ruler who will appear on the world scene just before the establishment of Christ's kingdom. What specific qualities can you see in Antiochus that you might also expect to see in an evil ruler bent on world conquest?

---

10. In what ways would this chapter be an encouragement to Christians living under political tyranny (or even emotional discouragement or spiritual attack)?

---

11. How does this chapter fit with Daniel's main theme of God's sovereignty?

---

12. What perspective does this chapter give us in undertanding how a good God can permit evil?

10
Prayer and Prediction
Daniel 9

One morning, shortly after the Medes and the Persians had conquered Babylon, Daniel was reading the book of the prophet Jeremiah. Jeremiah had been a prophet in Jerusalem when Daniel was a boy. As he read the prophet's words, a couple of passages seemed to leap off the page (Jer 25:8-12; 29:10-11). God promised that Israel's captivity would last seventy years, and then God would bring them back to the land. Daniel began to add up the years since his deportation and realized that the captivity was almost over! As Daniel's mind was gripped by the written Word of God, the urge to pray was born. God's answer to Daniel's prayer was swift—and surprising! This passage not only teaches us about Daniel's response to God's Word; we also learn how we should respond to God's promises to us.

---

1. In times of deep personal crisis, men and women are often driven to pray. If you have experienced such a time in your life, briefly describe what it was like.

---

2. Read Daniel 9. If God had already promised to release the nation after seventy years of captivity, why did Daniel have to pray? (Jeremiah 29:10-15 might give you some insight.)

3. In verses 4-19, which aspects of God's character did Daniel appeal to as the basis of his requests?

---

4. Daniel also appealed to God on the basis of specific actions of grace and judgment God had performed for Israel. Which acts did he refer to, and why do you think he chose these particular ones?

---

5. What failures of the nation are identified as the cause for God's judgment?

---

6. Daniel consistently uses the plural pronoun *we* throughout the prayer. Why do you think Daniel could confess for the whole nation?

Why does he include himself in the confession?

---

7. What specific insights about your prayer life can you glean from Daniel's prayer?

8. In verse 24 Gabriel mentions six things that will happen for the people of Israel and the holy city of Jerusalem within seventy "sevens" (usually interpreted as 490 years; see Lev 25:8-24). What do you think these things mean individually and collectively?

---

9. The 490-year clock begins with a "decree to restore and rebuild Jerusalem" (v. 25). This probably refers to either Cyrus's decree to rebuild the temple in 539 B.C. (Ezra 1:1-4) or Artaxerxes' decree to rebuild the city in 444 B.C. (Neh 2:1-10). In your opinion, which of these decrees best fits the stipulations of verse 25? Explain.

---

10. Gabriel states that once the decree is issued, there will be seven "sevens" and sixty-two "sevens" (483 years?) until the Anointed One comes and is "cut off" (vv. 25-26). Those who take the earlier date for the decree usually interpret the 483 years symbolically. They simply refer to an unspecified period of time until the Messiah comes and all is restored. Those who take the later date for the decree note that 483 years after 444 B.C. is A.D. 33, the date of Christ's triumphal entry into Jerusalem.* Which of these interpretations do you prefer, and why?

---

*The calculation is based on a 360-day "prophetic year" (see Rev 11:2-3; 12:6, 14; 13:5). When adding these prophetic years to 444 B.C., it is necessary to add one additional year because there is no A.D. 0.

11. Verse 26 states that "the people of the ruler who will come will destroy the city and the sanctuary." The Romans destroyed Jerusalem and its temple in A.D. 70. According to verse 27, how would you describe the course of events during the final "seven," or period of seven years?

---

12. The evil Roman ruler has been prefigured by such people as Antiochus IV and the Emperor Nero. But the New Testament speaks of his coming as still future (2 Thess 2:1-4). How do you react to the possibility of this wicked world ruler arising in our generation?

What does this chapter offer you (if anything) in the face of such a possibility?

11

Another Vision of the Future

Daniel 10:1—11:35

Wars, terrorism, assassinations—so often world events seem out of control. We are frustrated and frightened because of our inability to do anything to stop them. The last of four great visions given to Daniel presents God's perspective on world events.

1. What recent national or international crisis made you feel insecure or frightened? Explain.

2. Read Daniel 10:1—11:1. Passover and the Feast of Unleavened Bread took place in the first month of the year, from the 14th to the 21st. Why was Daniel mourning and fasting when traditionally Jews feasted and gave thanks for God's deliverance out of Egypt?

3. Why did the vision of verses 4-6 cause Daniel to react the way he did (vv. 7-11)?

4. What do the angel's words to Daniel tell us about God's response to those who seek him (vv. 12-14)?

---

5. How might Daniel's experience encourage us to be persistent in prayer?

---

6. When Daniel mentions "the prince of the Persian kingdom" (v. 13) who resisted God's messenger, he probably means an evil spirit who influenced the affairs of the Persian government. What does this "unveiling" of demonic activity in political affairs teach us about our modern world?

---

7. If an evil power could hinder an angel in Daniel's day, what does this indicate about our own need for help against Satan's forces?

---

8. Read 11:2-35. The conflict between Persia and Greece is described in verses 2-4. Based on your previous studies in Daniel, what names and events can you match with these predictions?

---

9. Verses 5-35 are concerned with the conflict between the Syrian division of the Greek empire ruled by the Seleucid family ("the king of the North") and the Egyptian division of the Greek empire ruled by the Ptolemies ("the king of the South"). Their various rivalries and intrigues are outlined with amazing accuracy.

The focus of the passage is on a man we have met in Daniel before—Antiochus Epiphanes. Verses 21-24 describe his conquest of the people of Israel who had regathered in Palestine after the exile. What do we learn from these verses about Antiochus' character and methods of operation?

---

10. Antiochus invaded Egypt the first time with relative success (vv. 25-28). The second time he met some new opposition and in his frustration vented his anger on "the holy covenant," the Jewish religion (vv. 29-31). What can we learn from verses 32-35 about why God may allow genuine believers to suffer under the hand of a godless tyrant?

---

11. All of chapter 11 was *future* to Daniel. However, verses 2-35 are *past* to us. Looking back, we can see how precisely God's predictions came true. One scholar has calculated that, in the first thirty-five verses of this chapter, 135 specific prophecies are made that were literally fulfilled. How does this support the theme of the book—that the Lord is sovereign over history?

---

12. How can God's sovereign rule help us to stand firm when evil seems to triumph?

12
A Dark Day and a Brilliant End for God's People
Daniel 11:36—12:13

We come to the end of our journey through Daniel with mixed feelings. We are glad to be at our destination, but we will miss Daniel's close presence. I hope as a result of this study you have a new appreciation for the sovereign majesty of God—a God who can predict the future in detail, a God who raises up kings and kingdoms and who also brings them to ruin, a God who can protect Daniel in the lion's den, and a God who is just as concerned about us and our lives.

The second part of Daniel's final prophetic vision in 11:36—12:13 projects Daniel far into the future to "the time of the end" of world history. The vision focuses on the nation of Israel, but gives us strong encouragement and hope during difficult times.

---

1. Read Daniel 11:36—12:13. Building from the prototype of the antichrist in Antiochus Epiphanes (11:21-32), the heavenly messenger now describes the final oppressor of Israel who will arise at "the time of the end" (vv. 35-40). This "king," following the example of Antiochus, will magnify himself as a god. How would you describe the "religious" character and actions of this king from verses 36-37?

2. The antichrist's god will be "a god of fortresses"—the ancient god of war and militarism (vv. 38-39). How do we see the influence of this "god" at work today?

3. From verses 40-43 trace the military career of this future king.

4. "Reports from the east and the north" (v. 44) which alarm the king are apparently reports of other armies marching toward Israel ("at the beautiful holy mountain") for a final climactic battle. How would you describe the outcome of this battle from what you are told in this passage and from what you have already learned about the antichrist earlier in Daniel (such as 7:11, 25-27)?

5. The king's defeat and the deliverance of the godly comes through the intervention of Michael, "the great prince" (12:1). How do you envision this intervention will take place?

6. How can this victory and the messenger's description of the resurrection (vv. 1-3) encourage us during times of tribulation or persecution?

7. Why do you think Daniel is given the instruction to seal the scroll "until the time of the end" (vv. 4, 9)?

8. Daniel's natural question after seeing this vision is "How long will it be before these astonishing things are fulfilled?" (v. 6). How would you paraphrase the answer he received in verse 7?

---

9. In verses 9-13, do you think the messenger avoided Daniel's last question (v. 8) or did he answer it? Explain.

---

10. As you think back over the book of Daniel, what specific aspect of Daniel's character or example helped you most to live spiritually in a secular world?

How did it help you?

---

11. In the course of your study in Daniel, what did you learn about the character of God that strengthened you most spiritually?

How has this helped you to worship and trust God more fully?

Leader's Notes

Leading a Bible discussion can be an enjoyable and rewarding experience. But it can also be *scary*—especially if you've never done it before. If this is your feeling, you're in good company. When God asked Moses to lead the Israelites out of Egypt, he replied, "O Lord, please send someone else to do it!" (Ex 4:13).

When Solomon became king of Israel, he felt the task was far beyond his abilities. "I am only a little child and do not know how to carry out my duties. . . . Who is able to govern this great people of yours?" (1 Kings 3:7, 9).

When God called Jeremiah to be a prophet, he replied, "Ah, Sovereign LORD, . . . I do not know how to speak; I am only a child" (Jer 1:6).

The list goes on. The apostles were "unschooled, ordinary men" (Acts 4:13). Timothy was young, frail and frightened. Paul's "thorn in the flesh" made him feel weak. But God's response to all of his servants—including you—is essentially the same: "My grace is sufficient for you" (2 Cor 12:9). Relax. God helped these people in spite of their weaknesses, and he can help you in spite of your feelings of inadequacy.

There is another reason why you should feel encouraged. Leading a Bible discussion is not difficult if you follow certain guidelines. You don't need to be an expert on the Bible or a trained teacher. The suggestions listed below should enable you to effectively and enjoyably fulfill your role as leader.

Preparing to Lead

1. Ask God to help you understand and apply the passage to your own life. Unless this happens, you will not be prepared to lead others. Pray too for the various members of the group. Ask God to give you an enjoyable and profitable time together studying his Word.

2. As you begin each study, read and reread the assigned Bible passage to familiarize yourself with what the author is saying. In the case of book studies, you may want to read through the entire book prior to the first study. This will give you a helpful overview of its contents.

3. This study guide is based on the New International Version of the Bible. It will help you and the group if you use this translation as the basis for your study and discussion. Encourage others to use the NIV also, but allow them the freedom to use whatever translation they prefer.

4. Carefully work through each question in the study. Spend time in meditation and reflection as you formulate your answers.

5. Write your answers in the space provided in the study guide. This will help you to express your understanding of the passage clearly.

6. It might help you to have a Bible dictionary handy. Use it to look up any unfamiliar words, names or places.

7. Once you have finished your own study of the passage, familiarize yourself with the leader's notes for the study you are leading. These are designed to help you in several ways. First, they tell you the purpose the study guide author had in mind while writing the study. Take time to think through how the study questions work together to accomplish that purpose. Second, the notes provide you with additional background information or comments on some of the questions. This information can be useful if people have difficulty understanding or answering a question. Third, the leader's notes can alert you to potential problems you may encounter during the study.

8. If you wish to remind yourself of anything mentioned in the leader's notes, make a note to yourself below that question in the study.

Leading the Study

1. Begin the study on time. Unless you are leading an evangelistic Bible study, open with prayer, asking God to help you to understand and apply the passage.

2. Be sure that everyone in your group has a study guide. Encourage them to prepare beforehand for each discussion by working through the questions in the guide.

3. At the beginning of your first time together, explain that these studies are meant to be discussions not lectures. Encourage the members of the group to participate. However, do not put pressure on those who may be hesitant to speak during the first few sessions.

4. Read the introductory paragraph at the beginning of the discussion. This will orient the group to the passage being studied.

5. Read the passage aloud if you are studying one chapter or less. You may choose to do this yourself, or someone else may read if he or she has been asked to do so prior to the study. Longer passages may occasionally be read in parts at different times during the study. Some studies may cover several chapters. In such cases reading aloud would probably take too much time, so the group members should simply read the assigned passages prior to the study.

6. As you begin to ask the questions in the guide, keep several things in mind. First, the questions are designed to be used just as they are written. If you wish, you may simply read them aloud to the group. Or you may prefer to express them in your own words. However, unnecessary rewording of the questions is not recommended.

Second, the questions are intended to guide the group toward understanding and applying the *main idea* of the passage. The author of the guide has stated his or her view of this central idea in the *purpose* of the study in the leader's notes. You should try to understand how the passage expresses this idea and how the study questions work together to lead the group in that direction.

There may be times when it is appropriate to deviate from the study guide. For example, a question may have already been answered. If so, move on to the next question. Or someone may raise an important question not covered in the guide. Take time to discuss it! The important thing is to use discretion. There may be many routes you can travel to reach the goal of the study. But the easiest route is usually the one the author has suggested.

7. Avoid answering your own questions. If necessary, repeat or rephrase them until they are clearly understood. An eager group quickly becomes passive and silent if they think the leader will do most of the talking.

8. Don't be afraid of silence. People may need time to think about the question before formulating their answers.

9. Don't be content with just one answer. Ask, "What do the rest of you think?" or "Anything else?" until several people have given answers to the question.

10. Acknowledge all contributions. Try to be affirming whenever possible. Never reject an answer. If it is clearly wrong, ask, "Which verse led you to that conclusion?" or again, "What do the rest of you think?"

11. Don't expect every answer to be addressed to you, even though this will probably happen at first. As group members become more at ease, they will begin to truly interact with each other. This is one sign of a healthy discussion.

12. Don't be afraid of controversy. It can be very stimulating. If you don't resolve an issue completely, don't be frustrated. Move on and keep it in mind for later. A subsequent study may solve the problem.

13. Stick to the passage under consideration. It should be the source for answering the questions. Discourage the group from unnecessary cross-referencing. Likewise, stick to the subject and avoid going off on tangents.

14. Periodically summarize what the *group* has said about the passage. This helps to draw together the various ideas mentioned and gives continuity to the study. But don't preach.

15. Conclude your time together with conversational prayer. Be sure to ask God's help to apply those things which you learned in the study.

16. End on time.

Components of Small Groups

A healthy small group should do more than study the Bible. There are four components you should consider as you structure your time together.

Nurture. Being a part of a small group should be a nurturing and edifying experience. You should grow in your knowledge and love of God and each other. If we are to properly love God, we must know and keep his commandments (Jn 14:15). That is why Bible study should be a foundational part of your small group. But you can be nurtured by other things as well. You can memorize Scripture, read and discuss a book, or occasionally listen to a tape of a good speaker.

Community. Most people have a need for close friendships. Your small group can be an excellent place to cultivate such relationships. Allow time for informal interaction before and after the study. Have a time of sharing during the meeting. Do fun things together as a group, such as a potluck supper or a picnic. Have someone bring refreshments to the meeting. Be creative!

Worship. A portion of your time together can be spent in worship and prayer. Praise God together for who he is. Thank him for what he has done and is doing in your lives and in the world. Pray for each other's needs. Ask God to help you to apply what you have learned. Sing hymns together.

Mission. Many small groups decide to work together in some form of outreach. This can be a practical way of applying what you have learned. You can host a series of evangelistic discussions for your friends or neighbors. You can visit people at a home for the elderly. Help a widow with cleaning or repair jobs around her home. Such projects can have a transforming influence on your group.

For a detailed discussion of the nature and function of small groups, read *Small Group Leaders' Handbook* (IVP, Downers Grove) or *Good Things Come in Small Groups* (Scripture Union).

General Suggestions for Studies 1-7 (Dan 1—6)

Daniel's life and character provide help to those of us who are trying to live a distinctively Christian life in the context of a pagan, secular society. The theme of godly living in an ungodly world is the focus in each of these studies. The application questions particularly have been formulated with that central concept in mind. Therefore, as you lead a group it is important to apply the spiritual principles in as many ways as possible to the individual cultural context of your group—a university campus, an office complex, the business or professional world, your neighborhood. "How does Daniel's example change *my* life?" should be the underlying question in each group session.

These narrative chapters are not difficult to understand. Their value in spiritual growth will become evident as the truths they teach are lived out. You as the leader, then, should strive to keep the study from becoming simply an academic analysis of ancient events. Instead, you should push for both clear understanding of what God's Word says *and* how it should affect the people in your study group.

As mentioned in the introduction, some scholars have denied the authenticity and prophetic integrity of the book of Daniel. The group leader should have at least a basic understanding of the arguments raised against Daniel and how other scholars have defended the historicity of the book. Very helpful information can be found in:

Josh McDowell, *Daniel in the Critics' Den* (San Bernardino, Calif.: Campus Crusade for Christ, 1979).

Roland K. Harrison, *Introduction to the Old Testament* (Leicester: Inter-Varsity Press, 1969),"The Book of Daniel," pp.1105-34.

Robert Dick Wilson, *Studies in the Book of Daniel,* vols. 1 and 2 (Grand Rapids, Mich.: Baker Book House, 1979).

You may also want to read a good commentary as a supplement to your study. Some suggested commentaries are:

Joyce Baldwin, *Daniel* (Leicester: InterVarsity Press, 1978).

Ronald S. Wallace, *The Message of Daniel* (Leicester: InterVarsity Press, 1979).

Press, 1979).
John C. Whitcomb, *Daniel*, Everyman's Bible Commentary (Chicago: Moody Press, 1985).
Leon Wood, *A Commentary on Daniel* (Grand Rapids, Mich.: Zondervan, 1973).

Study 1. Have You Got What It Takes? Daniel 1.
Purpose: To be challenged with the importance of taking a stand for biblical truth and personal conviction.

You should be thoroughly familiar with the introduction to the study guide. It might be profitable to give a brief summary of the historical context of Daniel, perhaps by using a time line to visualize the main events.

Question 2. Since God's sovereign authority is such a dominant theme in the book of Daniel, it is important to note the author's basic presuppositions. These verses set the tone for the rest of the book.

Question 3. Daniel's Hebrew name meant "God is my Judge." His new Babylonian name, Belteshazzar, meant "May Bel protect the king." (Bel was the chief Babylonian deity.)

The Jewish historian, Josephus, tells us that Daniel and the other young men were also made eunuchs. This was so they could function in the king's own household without fear that they would become sexually involved with any of the king's wives.

The word translated "youths" in verse 4 is normally used to refer to a young teen-ager, twelve to fourteen years old. Daniel had to have been quite young, since seventy-three years later he was still alive and active (Dan 10:1).

Question 8. The king's food produced two problems for Daniel and his godly friends. First, it was the custom of the king to offer his food to idols before it was eaten. Daniel viewed eating that food as the first step toward spiritual compromise. Second, the diet would have included foods that God had declared to be unclean for his people. Pork was a delicacy in Babylon. Horse meat was commonly eaten. Both were prohibited (see Lev 11:2-8). So rather than offend God, Daniel made up his mind not to become defiled.

Question 9. Notice that verses 9 and 17 give God the ultimate credit for their abilities and success.

Study 2. A Disturbing Dream. Daniel 2:1-30.
Purpose: To demonstrate God's faithfulness to us in a time of personal crisis.

Question 2. The four groups of men referred to in Daniel 2:2 who were summoned by Nebuchadnezzar made up the king's "cabinet." They were his advisers in matters of state. They were also closely connected with the Babylonian religious system and claimed to have the ability to predict the future. All these men were deeply involved in the occult. It is significant that Daniel makes a clear distinction between the methods of the occultic priests and his reliance on truth revealed to him by the true God (see 2:27-28).

Verse 1 says that this was in the second year of Nebuchadnezzar's reign. He became the king just after his conquest of Jerusalem in 605 B.C. Therefore, this was also the second year of Daniel's training.

Question 4. Be sure the group discusses how Daniel's "wisdom and tact" (v. 14) are demonstrated in this crisis.

Study 3. The Future from a Divine Perspective. Daniel 2:31-49.

Purpose: To make clear God's future program as it was revealed to Daniel.

The main problem the leader may face in this study is the clash between various schools of thought on end-time events. The key interpretive disagreement centers on where the church age "fits" in the flow of earthly kingdoms represented in the statue. Focus the group's attention on the particular prophetic passage covered in the study and do not let the group study become a "bull session" about entire systems of prophetic thought.

Question 5. This identification of the kingdoms seems most likely since Media and Persia are viewed as *one* kingdom rather than two in 8:20, and the next kingdom is identified as Greece in 8:21. However, some interpreters have identified the kingdoms as Media (silver), Persia (bronze) and Greece (iron).

Question 7. The second part of this question could also be controversial. Don't spend too much time here. Daniel doesn't give us a complete answer.

Study 4. Bow or Burn! Daniel 3.

Purpose: To understand the risks and rewards of obedience to God and his Word.

Question 2. It isn't possible to prove a connection between the statue in chapter 2 and the image in chapter 3, but such a connection seems likely. In chapter 2 Nebuchadnezzar was only the head of gold. Other kingdoms would eventually replace his, and God's kingdom would ultimately be supreme. Perhaps this thought irritated Nebuchadnezzar, who probably wanted to think his own kingdom would be everlasting. In response (perhaps), he builds an image in chapter 3 that is gold from head to foot. Is this a challenge to what God had declared? Let the group decide!

The dimensions of this image may raise some questions. The text says that the image was "ninety feet high and nine feet wide." Those dimensions would produce a very grotesque statue. It would be comparable to a person who was six feet tall and seven inches wide! It's most probable that the image stood on a base and that the total height (base + statue) was ninety feet. Archaeologists have discovered a brick pedestal just six miles south of the site of ancient Babylon in a place called Tolul Dura ("mounds of Dura"). The pedestal ruin is forty-five feet square and twenty feet high. The French archaeologist who discovered it, Julius Oppert, believed that it was the base of the image described in Daniel 3.

Question 3. Another question raised in connection with this account is: Where was Daniel? Certainly Daniel would not have bowed to Nebuchadnezzar's image. Why wasn't he thrown into the fire with his three friends? We aren't told in the passage, so we don't know for sure. Daniel, however, did hold a high rank in the empire (see Dan 2:48) and could well have been absent on official business.

Question 11. Seek to have the members of the group express specific steps they can take to prepare themselves mentally and spiritually for handling challenges to their faith.

Study 5. The Sovereign God Rules. Daniel 4.

Purpose: To show that God is sovereign over our lives and that he humbles those who are proud.

Question 5. This question will probably generate considerable discussion. You might point out that God does not cause moral evil. It does not originate from him. But he does permit it to exist and to continue for his purposes. You should also point out that God will judge unrepentant leaders for their sin. Divine sovereignty does not erase human responsibility. Nebuchadnezzar is the prime example of that truth!

Question 8. The medical term for Nebuchadnezzar's condition is *boanthropy*—a rare condition in which the person behaves like a bull or a cow. An eyewitness observation of a person in such a condition is given in Roland Harrison, *Introduction to the Old Testament* (Leicester: Inter-Varsity Press, 1969), pp.1116-17.

Study 6. The Handwriting on the Wall. Daniel 5.

Purpose: To see the role the committed Christian can play in speaking to a decaying society.

Question 2. Shortly after Nebuchadnezzar's return to sanity (described in last verses of chapter 4), he died in 562 B.C. The events in chapter 5 took place in 539 B.C., twenty-three years later.

In 556 B.C., a king named Nabonidus took the throne and reigned for the last twenty-five years of the empire's existence. He was the king when the city fell to the Persians. Critical scholars have been quick to point to Daniel's "error" in verse 1 when he writes of "King Belshazzar." For over two thousand years no record of Belshazzar was found. In the early 1900s, however, archaeologists began to dig up the ruins of ancient Babylon. Amazingly the name *Bel-shar-utsur* (Belshazzar) began to appear. Finally a British archaeologist published an inscription from Babylon that said Belshazzar was the son of Nabonidus. Furthermore, because Nabonidus liked to travel so much, he entrusted the kingship to Belshazzar in 553 B.C. Belshazzar was the coregent with Nabonidus for fourteen years. That also explains why Belshazzar offered to make Daniel "*third* highest ruler in the kingdom" (v. 7). Instead of being a mistake, the reference to Belshazzar demonstrates the accuracy of Daniel's book.

Question 3. Belshazzar's confidence rested on the fortifications of the city of Babylon. The walled part of the city was sixty miles in circumference. The wall itself was 150 feet high and 87 feet thick. Four chariots could ride abreast on top of the wall. Around the wall was a thirty-foot moat. The city was considered impregnable.

This source of Babylonian smugness became their downfall. Fresh water was supplied to Babylon by a canal from the river Euphrates that flowed through the city. According to Herodotus, the Persian army dug another canal to divert the water. On the night of Belshazzar's feast, they opened the new canal and marched into Babylon on the riverbed. There was almost no struggle. While the Babylonian soldiers slept and Belshazzar feasted, the Medes and the Persians conquered the impregnable city.

Question 5. The words written on the wall were normal Aramaic words. The wise men could read them ("measured, measured, weighed, divided in two") but could not explain their significance or meaning. Only Daniel had access to God's "commentary"!

Study 7. On the Menu at the Lions' Club. Daniel 6.

Purpose: To encourage Christians to persevere in their commitments to the Lord in spite of opposition or oppression.

Question 2. The main critical question in chapter 6 is the identity of Darius the Mede. He was apparently the man to whom Cyrus, the Persian monarch, entrusted the area around Babylon. Daniel refers to Darius as "the king." Darius reorganized the government under Persian authority. Because of his wisdom, Daniel was included in the top leadership of the new government.

Question 8. The lions' den was not an unusual means of execution in the ancient Near East. Lions were kept half-starved in an underground network of caverns. Victims were dropped in from a hole in the top to be ripped to shreds. Some question may be raised as to why the wives and children of the conspirators were thrown into the lions' den. It was the custom of ancient pagan kings to eliminate the entire family of anyone perceived as an enemy.

General Suggestions for Studies 8-12 (Dan 7—12)

The second part of the book of Daniel focuses on Daniel's prophetic visions. As explained in the introduction, the interpretation of these prophecies has been the source of much debate among believers. You should not allow the group session to become a debate over which system of interpretation is correct. The questions center on the text itself, and that is where the discussion should center. You also need to be on guard to your own presuppositions. Don't be guilty of promoting your own pet view, either! The purpose of the group discussion is to understand Daniel's message and to apply that message to our lives. While these chapters are more difficult than the first six, they are no less powerful in their impact on those who seek to understand them.

Study 8. A Prophetic Panorama. Daniel 7.

Purpose: To instill confidence in God's plan for human history and in his power to do what he promises to do.

The visions recorded in chapters 7—12 were given at various times in Daniel's career. They are grouped together after the historical section because of their similarity in content. This vision fits historically between chapters 4 and 5 (approx. 553 B.C.).

Question 2. In most prophetic visions God communicates his message through symbolism. Nebuchadnezzar's vision of the "tree" in Daniel 4 is an example.

Question 3. As in all biblical parables and visions, not every minute detail is described. The important features of each beast are listed, and they parallel certain qualities of the kingdom each represents. Don't get bogged down in minor disagreements of interpretation.

The four beasts probably correspond to the four parts of the statue in

Daniel 2. The lion is the same as the head of gold (Babylon). The bear is the chest and arms of silver (Medo-Persia). The leopard is the belly and thighs of bronze (Greece). And the fourth beast is the same as the legs of iron (Rome).

Question 5. Jesus identified himself as this "son of man" in Mark 14:62.

Study 9. World Powers in Conflict. Daniel 8.

Purpose: To demonstrate how accurately God predicts the future and how precisely events fulfill what he declares will happen.

Questions 3-4. Some historical facts about the rivalry between the Greeks and the Persians will add depth to the symbolic descriptions given in these verses. A good commentary on Daniel will provide the needed background information.

Question 7. Antiochus Epiphanes is a key figure in this chapter and in chapter 11. This may be a good place to briefly sketch out the career of this man for the group.

Question 12. This chapter raises again "the problem of evil." God wants us to see that his plan for human history includes his sovereign permission and use of evil. Just because evil men seem to abound, we should not feel that God is absent or unconcerned.

Study 10. Prayer and Prediction. Daniel 9.

Purpose: To encourage the response of expectant prayer to God's promises.

Question 1. This study is a bit longer than the others, so be sure to pace the amount of time spent on each question.

Questions 8-12. This prophecy of "Daniel's seventy weeks" is probably the most widely debated prophecy in the book. Differing views abound. It is important, therefore, to discover the *primary* message of these verses rather than becoming involved in an endless debate about questions which at this time have no certain answers. Having said this, however, I should add that questions 8-12 are not designed to avoid the areas of dispute but rather to allow the group to wrestle with them and form their own conclusions.

Question 9. There are actually four decrees which have been suggested at one time or another as fulfilling the stipulations of verse 25. The other two are the decree of Darius in 519/18 B.C. (Ezra 6:1-12) and the decree of Artaxerxes to Ezra in 458/57 B.C. (Ezra 7:11-26). But the two decrees mentioned in question 9 seem to be the most likely candidates.

Question 10. Your group may become confused or frustrated with trying to solve the riddle of this prophecy. They should realize, however, that whether the years are taken symbolically or arithmetically many commentators agree that the prophecy refers to the coming of the Messiah. Just as God was in control of Israel's seventy-year captivity in Babylon, so he will be in control of Israel's future and will restore all things through the Messiah. These were strong words of hope to Daniel, as they are to us!

Study 11. Another Vision of the Future. Daniel 10:1—11:35.
Purpose: To assure believers that in spite of the opposition of men and of demons, God's plan for his people will be fulfilled.
Question 3. We do not know for certain the identify of the glorious being whom Daniel saw in his vision (10:4-6). Some Bible students have argued that it was the Lord Jesus. They claim a comparison of this passage with John's vision in Revelation 1:12-18 lends support to this view. Others have maintained that it was a mighty angel. Their contention is that Christ could not be resisted in his mission as this being was (cf. v. 13).
Question 4. This messenger was sent three weeks earlier—at the beginning of Daniel's fasting.
Question 6. The purpose of this question is not to lead the group into envisioning weird scenarios of demonic attack on our capital but to point out the very real influence exerted by Satan on national leaders. Some may reject the idea that demonic forces are at work today in the same way they were in Daniel's day. Some New Testament references to Satanic activity in the world (1 Jn 4:1-3; 5:19; Eph 2:2) and against Christians (Eph 6:11-12; 1 Pet 5:8-9; Jas 4:7) may help to answer that objection.
Question 9. The "ships of the western coastlands" (v. 30—the Hebrew term is used in some Old Testament passages to refer to the Romans) halted his march and made him turn around.

Study 12. A Dark Day and a Brilliant End for God's People. Daniel 11:36—12:13.
Purpose: To show the future history of Israel as they face great oppression by the antichrist and then final glorious deliverance by God.
Question 1. All attempts to fit the details of verses 40-45 into the known career of Antiochus Epiphanes have been futile. Those who make this identification simply assume these prophecies were never fulfilled. However, it is much better to see these verses as a description of the antichrist, who will arise at "the time of the end" (v. 35).
Question 3. Some commentators identify the antichrist as the king of the North. In my opinion, however, verse 40 indicates that the king of the North

and the king of the South will engage the antichrist in battle.

Questions 10-11. These questions are designed to give your group an overview of the entire study. Encourage them to share what the study of Daniel has meant to each of them personally.

Douglas Connelly is senior pastor of Calvary Bible Church in Kalamazoo, Michigan.